THE BLACKBERRY BLOSSOM FIDDLE BOOK SCORE AND PIANO ACCOMPANIMENT

Arrangements by Myanna Harvey

Exercises by Cassia Harvey

CHP387

©2020 by C. Harvey Publications All Rights Reserved.

www.charveypublications.com - print books
www.learnstrings.com - PDF downloadable books
www.harveystringarrangements.com - chamber music

Table of Contents

How to Use This Book..................................3
1. Harvest Home: First Warm-Up..................4
2. Harvest Home: Second Warm-Up.............5
3. Harvest Home...6
4. Blackberry Blossom: First Warm-Up..........8
5. Blackberry Blossom: Second Warm-Up.....9
6. Blackberry Blossom..................................10
7. The Dashing Sergeant: First Warm-Up.....12
8. The Dashing Sergeant: Second Warm-Up........13
9. The Dashing Sergeant............................14
10. Old Joe Clark: First Warm-Up..................16
11. Old Joe Clark: Second Warm-Up.............17
12. Old Joe Clark...18
13. King of the Fairies: First Warm-Up..........20
14. King of the Fairies: Second Warm-Up.....21
15. King of the Fairies................................22
16. The Blarney Pilgrim: First Warm-Up........24
17. The Blarney Pilgrim: Second Warm-Up...25
18. The Blarney Pilgrim..............................26
19. The Parting Blessing: Warm-Up...............28
20. The Parting Blessing............................29
21. Leather Breeches: First Warm-Up...........30
22. Leather Breeches: Second Warm-Up......31
23. Leather Breeches.................................32
24. The Rakes of Kildare: First Warm-Up......34
25. The Rakes of Kildare: Second Warm-Up........35
26. The Rakes of Kildare............................36
27. Big John McNeil: First Warm-Up.............38
28. Big John McNeil: Second Warm-Up........38
29. Big John McNeil...................................40
30. The Red-Haired Boy: First Warm-Up......42
31. The Red-Haired Boy: Second Warm-Up........43
32. The Red-Haired Boy.............................44

Full Score

1. Harvest Home: First Warm-Up..................46
2. Harvest Home: Second Warm-Up.............47
3. Harvest Home...48
4. Blackberry Blossom: First Warm-Up........52
5. Blackberry Blossom: Second Warm-Up....53
6. Blackberry Blossom................................54
7. The Dashing Sergeant: First Warm-Up.....58
8. The Dashing Sergeant: Second Warm-Up........59
9. The Dashing Sergeant...........................60
10. Old Joe Clark: First Warm-Up..................64
11. Old Joe Clark: Second Warm-Up.............65
12. Old Joe Clark...66
13. King of the Fairies: First Warm-Up..........70
14. King of the Fairies: Second Warm-Up.....71
15. King of the Fairies................................72
16. The Blarney Pilgrim: First Warm-Up........76
17. The Blarney Pilgrim: Second Warm-Up...77
18. The Blarney Pilgrim..............................78
19. The Parting Blessing: Warm-Up...............81
20. The Parting Blessing............................82
21. Leather Breeches: First Warm-Up...........84
22. Leather Breeches: Second Warm-Up......85
23. Leather Breeches.................................86
24. The Rakes of Kildare: First Warm-Up......90
25. The Rakes of Kildare: Second Warm-Up........91
26. The Rakes of Kildare............................92
27. Big John McNeil: First Warm-Up.............96
28. Big John McNeil: Second Warm-Up........97
29. Big John McNeil...................................98
30. The Red-Haired Boy: First Warm-Up......102
31. The Red-Haired Boy: Second Warm-Up........103
32. The Red-Haired Boy.............................104

How to Use This Series With Individual Students in Private Lessons
- Start by having yourE student play the Warm-Up Exercises. The "A" parts are more difficult than the "B" parts and can help them work towards the Advanced Melody on the next page.
- Have them play the Stress-Free Melody. Work on intonation and using quick, precise finger and bow changes.
- Have the student play the Advanced Melody. Start with small sections of 2-4 measures and then work to put them together to form the melody.
- Students can circle any places where they consistently stop and play two notes before and two notes after the stop, 5 times. They should start slowly and gradually get faster until they have thoroughly learned the transition.
- Have the student play the Stress-Free Melody and then the Advanced Melody while you play the Teacher Harmony on your instrument or the Piano Accompaniment.
- For some variety, switch parts with your student and have them try one of the Harmony parts.

How to Use This Book in a Mixed Instrument and/or Mixed-Level String Class
- The Violin, Viola, Cello, and Bass books can be played and learned together.
- Students at a moderately accomplished or more advanced level can play the Regular Exercise. Students at a basic or beginning level can play the Basic Exercise.
- Moderately accomplished students can play the Stress-Free Melody, more advanced students can play the Advanced Melody, and students at a basic or beginning level can play the Basic Harmony. The teacher can play any of the parts with the students, the Teacher Harmony, or the piano accompaniment.
- **The "A" and "B" parts of each exercise are compatible and can be played together.**
- **All melodies and harmonies for each fiddle tune are compatible and can be played together.**

How to Use This Book in a Small Chamber Group
- The Violin, Viola, Cello, and Bass books can be played and learned together.
- Warm up with the exercises and then play the fiddle tunes.
- Everyone can pick the part they feel most comfortable playing.
- Make sure at least one person is playing a melody part and at least one person is playing a harmony part. Feel free to play the teacher harmony part even if you are not a teacher!
- **The "A" and "B" parts of each exercise are compatible and can be played together.**
- **All melodies and harmonies for each fiddle tune are compatible and can be played together.**

Sample Order: How to Have Your Group Perform a Tune From This Book
Have students play the parts (A, B, etc.) listed for each time through the tune (1., 2., etc.)

| 1. A,B,C |
| 2. B,C |
| 3. A,C |

or

| 1. A,B,C,D |
| 2. B,C,D |
| 3. A,C,D |
| 4. A,B,C,D |

- Highlight the viola, cello, or bass parts by having everyone else play pizzicato on the harmony part.
- Performing with the piano accompaniment can help less-advanced groups center their intonation and stay together.

©2020 C. Harvey Publications All Rights Reserved.

1. Harvest Home: First Warm-Up

C. Harvey

Note: All page numbers in the piano accompaniment are the same as they are in the instrumental parts.

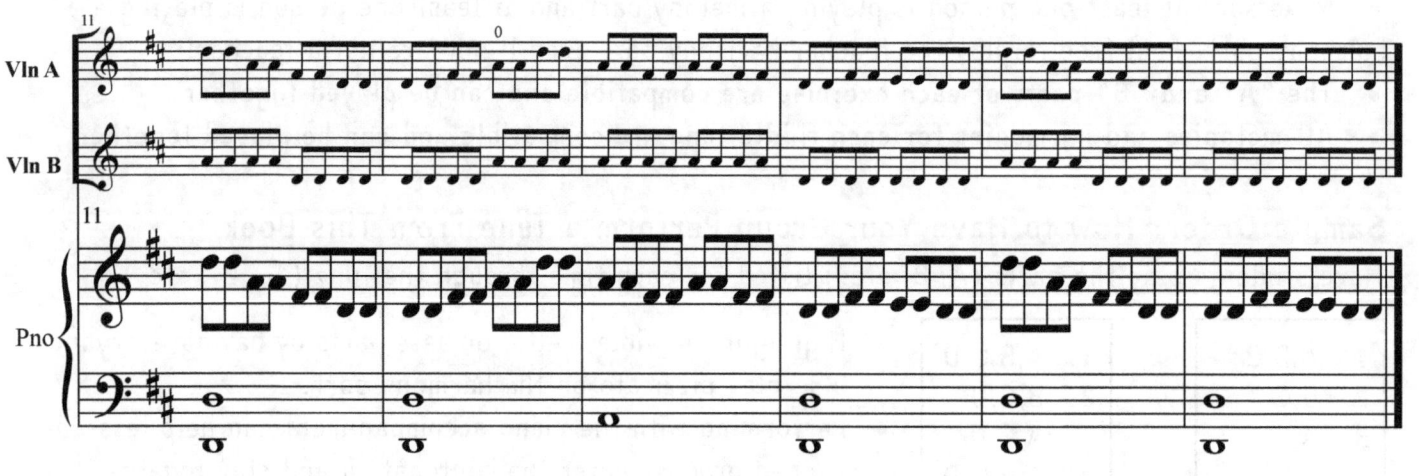

©2020 C. Harvey Publications All Rights Reserved.

2. Harvest Home: Second Warm-Up

3. Harvest Home

Trad., arr. M. Harvey

©2020 C. Harvey Publications All Rights Reserved.

The Blackberry Blossom Fiddle Book Score and Piano Accompaniment

©2020 C. Harvey Publications All Rights Reserved.

4. Blackberry Blossom: First Warm-Up

C. Harvey

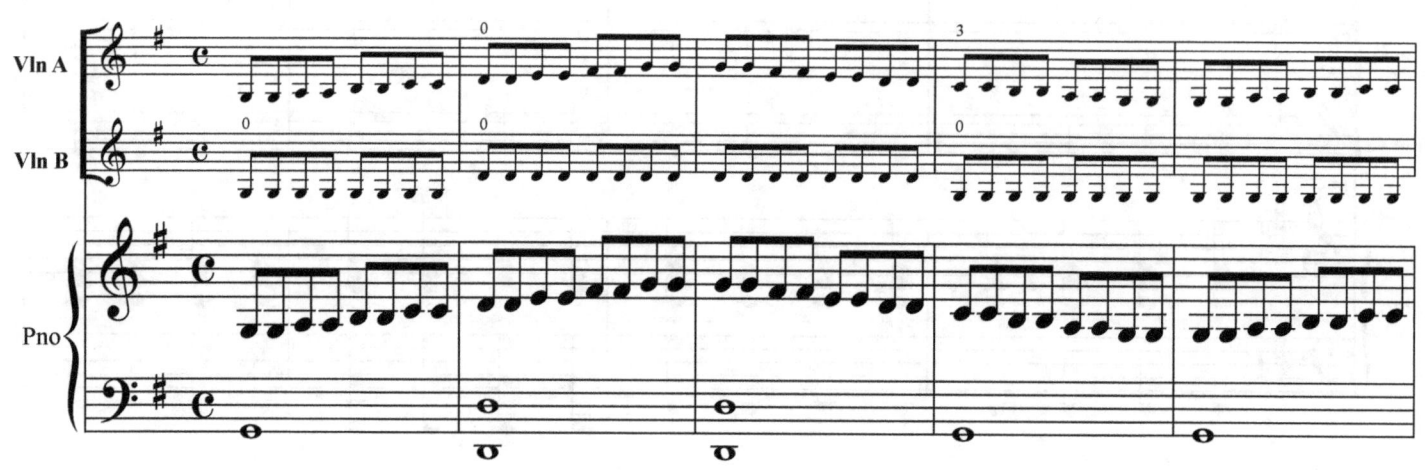

©2020 C. Harvey Publications All Rights Reserved.

5. Blackberry Blossom: Second Warm-Up

6. Blackberry Blossom

Trad., arr. M. Harvey

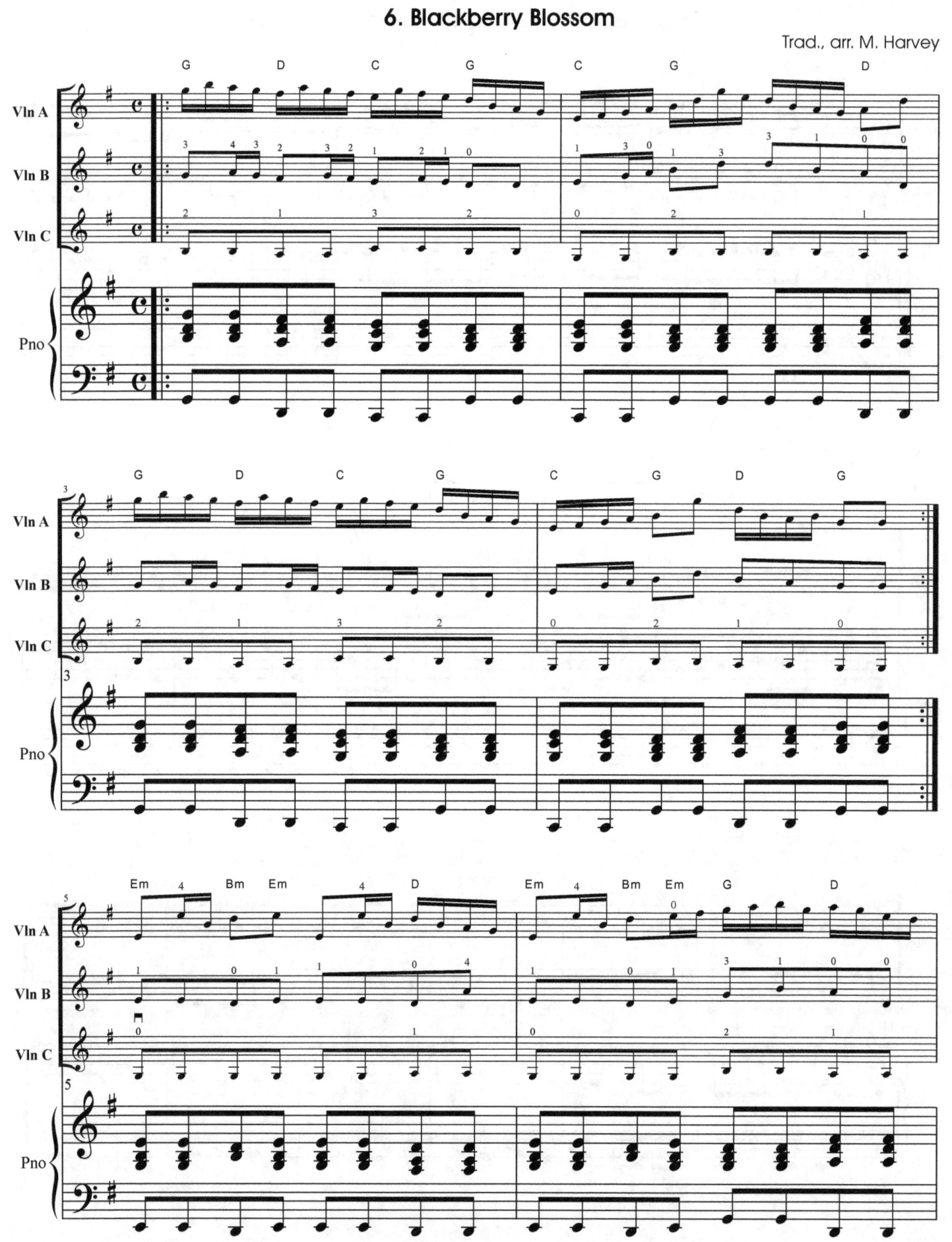

©2020 C. Harvey Publications All Rights Reserved.

The Blackberry Blossom Fiddle Book Score and Piano Accompaniment

©2020 C. Harvey Publications All Rights Reserved.

7. The Dashing Sergeant: First Warm-Up

C. Harvey

©2020 C. Harvey Publications All Rights Reserved.

8. The Dashing Sergeant: Second Warm-Up

9. The Dashing Sergeant

Trad., arr. M. Harvey

The Blackberry Blossom Fiddle Book Score and Piano Accompaniment

©2020 C. Harvey Publications All Rights Reserved.

10. Old Joe Clark: First Warm-Up

C. Harvey

©2020 C. Harvey Publications All Rights Reserved.

11. Old Joe Clark: Second Warm-Up

12. Old Joe Clark

Trad., arr. M. Harvey

The Blackberry Blossom Fiddle Book Score and Piano Accompaniment

13. King of the Fairies: First Warm-Up

C. Harvey

14. King of the Fairies: Second Warm-Up

15. King of the Fairies

Trad., arr. M. Harvey

The Blackberry Blossom Fiddle Book Score and Piano Accompaniment 23

©2020 C. Harvey Publications All Rights Reserved.

16. Blarney Pilgrim: First Warm-Up

C. Harvey

©2020 C. Harvey Publications All Rights Reserved.

17. Blarney Pilgrim: Second Warm-Up

18. Blarney Pilgrim

Trad., arr. M. Harvey

©2020 C. Harvey Publications All Rights Reserved.

The Blackberry Blossom Fiddle Book Score and Piano Accompaniment

©2020 C. Harvey Publications All Rights Reserved.

19. The Parting Blessing Warm-Up

C. Harvey

20. The Parting Blessing

Trad., arr. M. Harvey

Note: The A and B parts are the same in this tune.

©2020 C. Harvey Publications All Rights Reserved.

21. Leather Breeches: First Warm-Up

C. Harvey

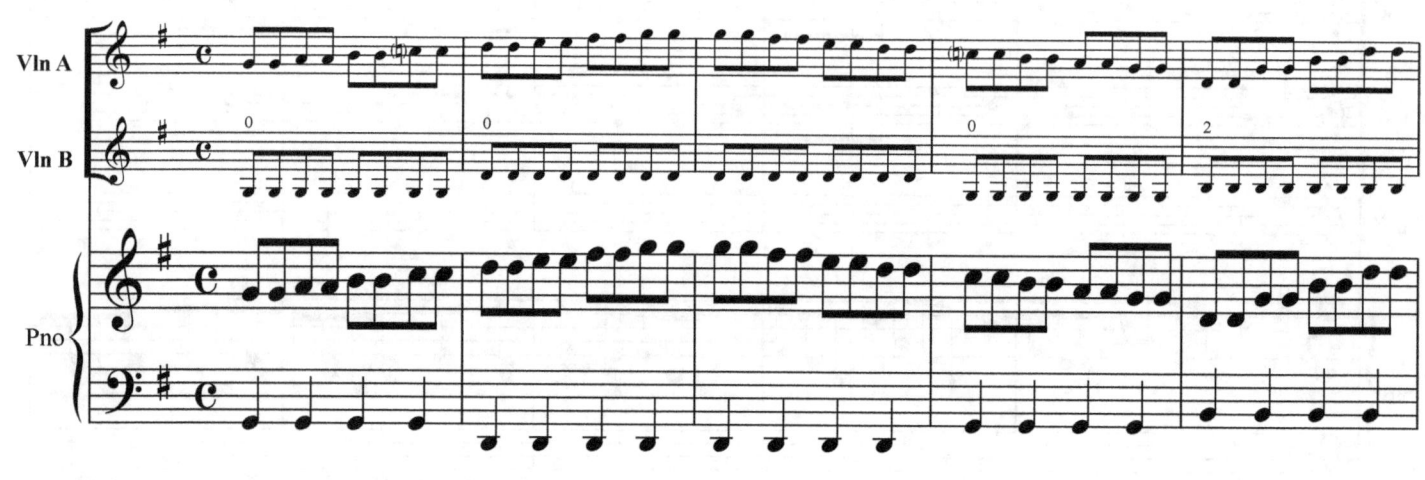

©2020 C. Harvey Publications All Rights Reserved.

22. Leather Breeches: Second Warm-Up

23. Leather Breeches

Trad., arr. M. Harvey

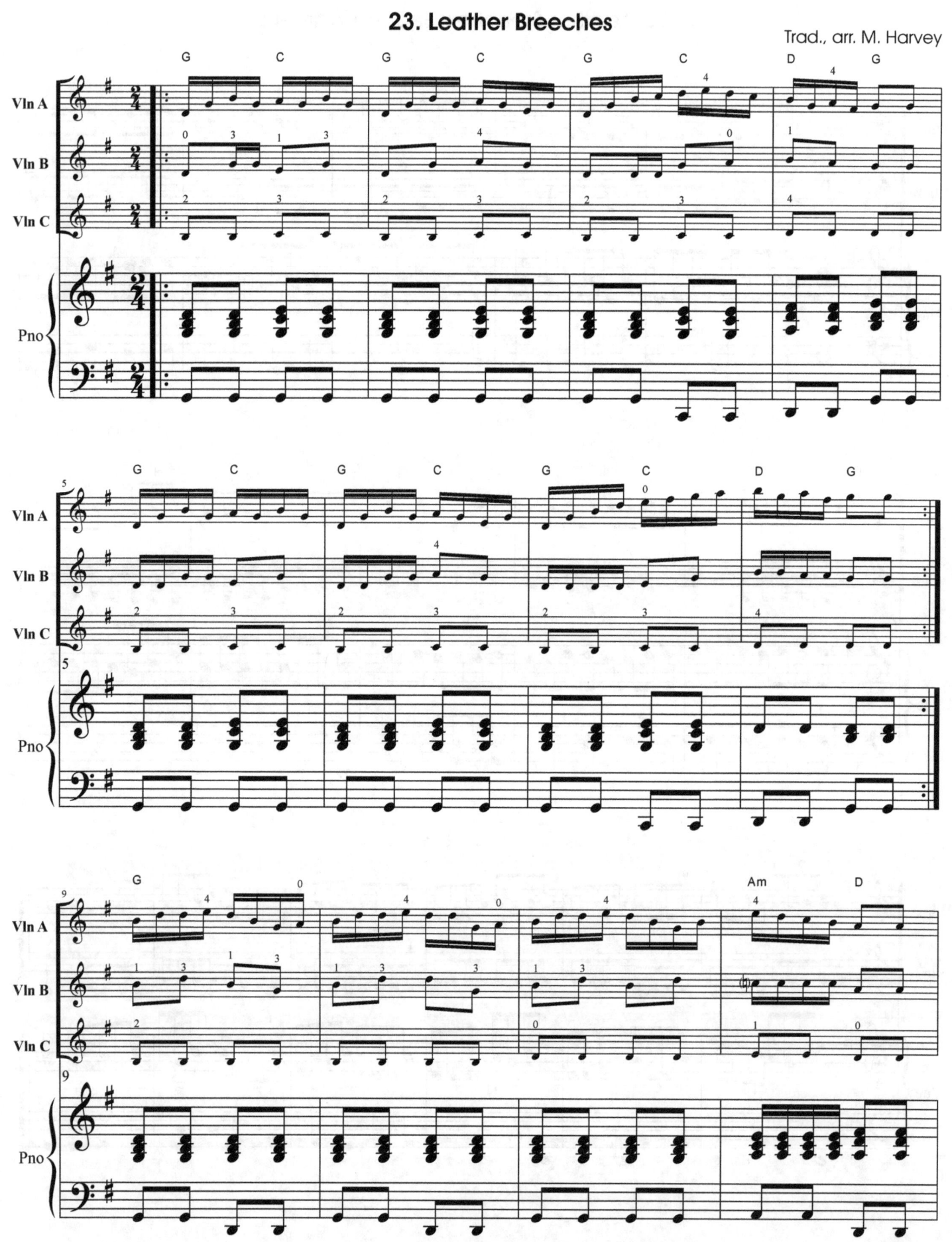

©2020 C. Harvey Publications All Rights Reserved.

24. The Rakes of Kildare: First Warm-Up

C. Harvey

25. The Rakes of Kildare: Second Warm-Up

26. The Rakes of Kildare

Trad., arr. M. Harvey

©2020 C. Harvey Publications All Rights Reserved.

The Blackberry Blossom Fiddle Book Score and Piano Accompaniment

©2020 C. Harvey Publications All Rights Reserved.

27. Big John McNeil: First Warm-Up

C. Harvey

©2020 C. Harvey Publications All Rights Reserved.

28. Big John McNeil: Second Warm-Up

29. Big John McNeil

Trad., arr. M. Harvey

©2020 C. Harvey Publications All Rights Reserved.

The Blackberry Blossom Fiddle Book Score and Piano Accompaniment

©2020 C. Harvey Publications All Rights Reserved.

30. Red-Haired Boy: First Warm-Up

C. Harvey

©2020 C. Harvey Publications All Rights Reserved.

31. Red-Haired Boy: Second Warm-Up

32. Red-Haired Boy

Trad., arr. M. Harvey

©2020 C. Harvey Publications All Rights Reserved.

The Blackberry Blossom Fiddle Book Score and Piano Accompaniment

©2020 C. Harvey Publications All Rights Reserved.

46 — The Blackberry Blossom Fiddle Book Score and Piano Accompaniment

Page 3 in instrumental books.

1. Harvest Home: First Warm-Up

C. Harvey

©2020 C. Harvey Publications   All Rights Reserved.

The Blackberry Blossom Fiddle Book Score and Piano Accompaniment

Page 4 in instrumental books.

2. Harvest Home: Second Warm-Up

©2020 C. Harvey Publications   All Rights Reserved.

3. Harvest Home

Page 5 in instrumental books.

Trad., arr. M. Harvey

©2020 C. Harvey Publications   All Rights Reserved.

The Blackberry Blossom Fiddle Book Score and Piano Accompaniment
49

©2020 C. Harvey Publications   All Rights Reserved.

50 The Blackberry Blossom Fiddle Book Score and Piano Accompaniment

©2020 C. Harvey Publications   All Rights Reserved.

The Blackberry Blossom Fiddle Book Score and Piano Accompaniment 51

©2020 C. Harvey Publications   All Rights Reserved.

4. Blackberry Blossom: First Warm-Up

Page 8 in instrumental books.

©2020 C. Harvey Publications   All Rights Reserved.

The Blackberry Blossom Fiddle Book Score and Piano Accompaniment

Page 9 in instrumental books.

5. Blackberry Blossom: Second Warm-Up

©2020 C. Harvey Publications   All Rights Reserved.

54

The Blackberry Blossom Fiddle Book Score and Piano Accompaniment

6. Blackberry Blossom

Page 10 in instrumental books.

Trad., arr. M. Harvey

©2020 C. Harvey Publications   All Rights Reserved.

The Blackberry Blossom Fiddle Book Score and Piano Accompaniment

©2020 C. Harvey Publications All Rights Reserved.

56 The Blackberry Blossom Fiddle Book Score and Piano Accompaniment

©2020 C. Harvey Publications All Rights Reserved.

The Blackberry Blossom Fiddle Book Score and Piano Accompaniment

58

Page 12 in instrumental books.

7. The Dashing Sergeant: First Warm-Up

The Blackberry Blossom Fiddle Book Score and Piano Accompaniment

©2020 C. Harvey Publications   All Rights Reserved.

The Blackberry Blossom Fiddle Book Score and Piano Accompaniment

Page 13 in instrumental books. **8. The Dashing Sergeant: Second Warm-Up**

©2020 C. Harvey Publications   All Rights Reserved.

60

The Blackberry Blossom Fiddle Book Score and Piano Accompaniment

9. The Dashing Sergeant

Page 14 in instrumental books.

Trad., arr. M. Harvey

©2020 C. Harvey Publications   All Rights Reserved.

The Blackberry Blossom Fiddle Book Score and Piano Accompaniment

61

©2020 C. Harvey Publications   All Rights Reserved.

62

The Blackberry Blossom Fiddle Book Score and Piano Accompaniment

©2020 C. Harvey Publications   All Rights Reserved.

The Blackberry Blossom Fiddle Book Score and Piano Accompaniment

©2020 C. Harvey Publications   All Rights Reserved.

64

Page 16 in instrumental books.

10. Old Joe Clark: First Warm-Up

The Blackberry Blossom Fiddle Book Score and Piano Accompaniment

©2020 C. Harvey Publications   All Rights Reserved.

The Blackberry Blossom Fiddle Book Score and Piano Accompaniment

Page 17 in instrumental books.

11. Old Joe Clark: Second Warm-Up

©2020 C. Harvey Publications   All Rights Reserved.

12. Old Joe Clark

Page 18 in instrumental books.

Trad., arr. M. Harvey

The Blackberry Blossom Fiddle Book Score and Piano Accompaniment 67

©2020 C. Harvey Publications All Rights Reserved.

68 The Blackberry Blossom Fiddle Book Score and Piano Accompaniment

©2020 C. Harvey Publications   All Rights Reserved.

The Blackberry Blossom Fiddle Book Score and Piano Accompaniment 69

©2020 C. Harvey Publications   All Rights Reserved.

13. King of the Fairies: First Warm-Up

Page 20 in instrumental books.

The Blackberry Blossom Fiddle Book Score and Piano Accompaniment 71

Page 21 in instrumental books. **14. King of the Fairies: Second Warm-Up**

©2020 C. Harvey Publications All Rights Reserved.

15. King of the Fairies

Page 22 in instrumental books.

Trad., arr. M. Harvey

©2020 C. Harvey Publications All Rights Reserved.

The Blackberry Blossom Fiddle Book Score and Piano Accompaniment

74 — The Blackberry Blossom Fiddle Book Score and Piano Accompaniment

©2020 C. Harvey Publications   All Rights Reserved.

The Blackberry Blossom Fiddle Book Score and Piano Accompaniment 75

©2020 C. Harvey Publications   All Rights Reserved.

76 The Blackberry Blossom Fiddle Book Score and Piano Accompaniment

Page 24 in instrumental books.

16. Blarney Pilgrim: First Warm-Up

©2020 C. Harvey Publications All Rights Reserved.

The Blackberry Blossom Fiddle Book Score and Piano Accompaniment

Page 25 in instrumental books.

17. Blarney Pilgrim: Second Warm-Up

©2020 C. Harvey Publications   All Rights Reserved.

78

Page 26 in instrumental books.

18. Blarney Pilgrim

Trad., arr. M. Harvey

©2020 C. Harvey Publications All Rights Reserved.

The Blackberry Blossom Fiddle Book Score and Piano Accompaniment

The Blackberry Blossom Fiddle Book Score and Piano Accompaniment 81

Page 28 in instrumental books.

19. The Parting Blessing Warm-Up

©2020 C. Harvey Publications   All Rights Reserved.

20. The Parting Blessing

Page 29 in instrumental books.

Trad., arr. M. Harvey

©2020 C. Harvey Publications   All Rights Reserved.

The Blackberry Blossom Fiddle Book Score and Piano Accompaniment 83

©2020 C. Harvey Publications   All Rights Reserved.

84

Page 30 in instrumental books.

21. Leather Breeches: First Warm-Up

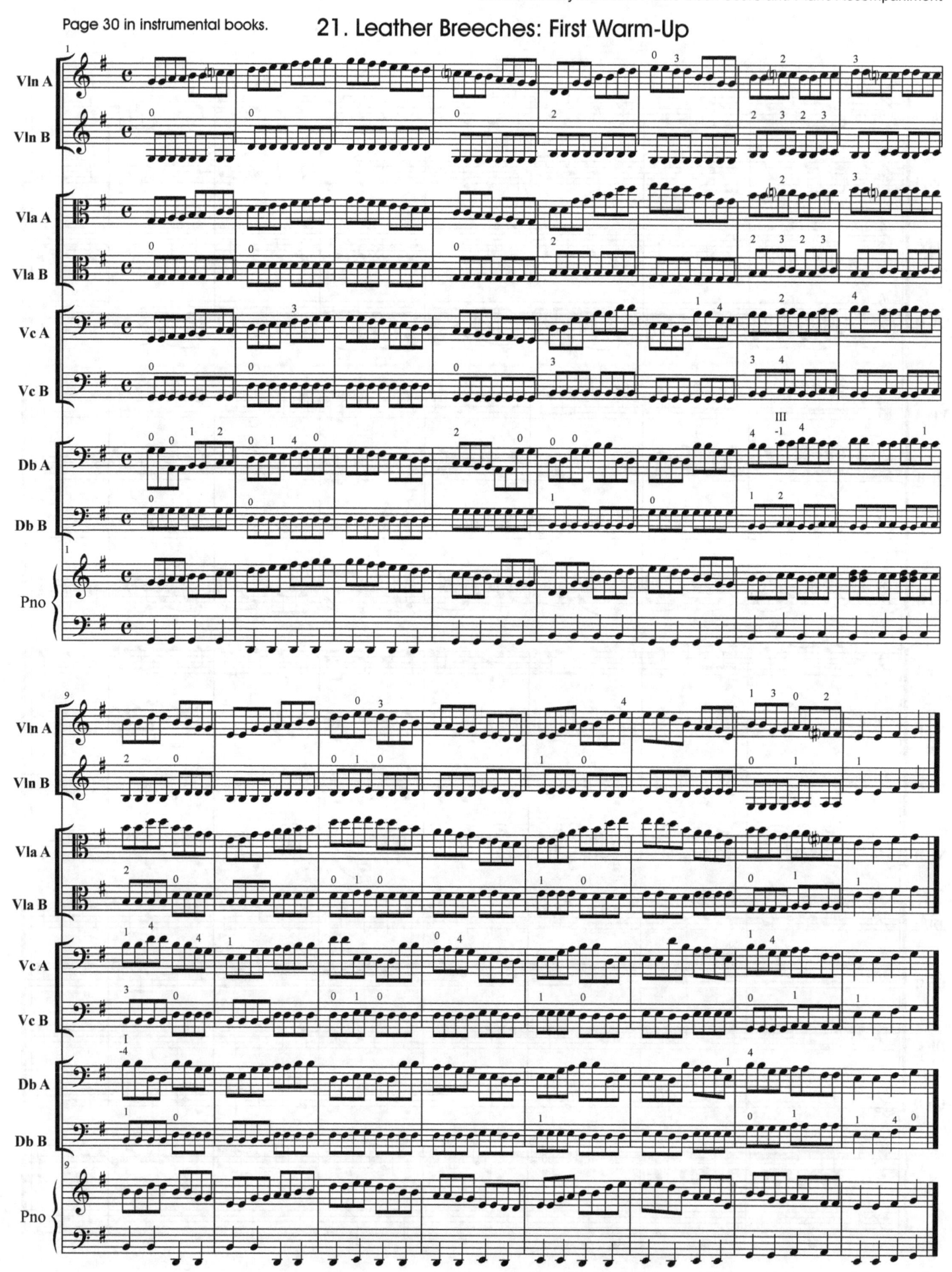

©2020 C. Harvey Publications   All Rights Reserved.

The Blackberry Blossom Fiddle Book Score and Piano Accompaniment

Page 31 in instrumental books.

22. Leather Breeches: Second Warm-Up

©2020 C. Harvey Publications   All Rights Reserved.

23. Leather Breeches

Page 32 in instrumental books.

Trad., arr. M. Harvey

©2020 C. Harvey Publications   All Rights Reserved.

The Blackberry Blossom Fiddle Book Score and Piano Accompaniment 87

©2020 C. Harvey Publications   All Rights Reserved.

24. The Rakes of Kildare: First Warm-Up

Page 34 in instrumental books.

The Blackberry Blossom Fiddle Book Score and Piano Accompaniment 91

Page 35 in instrumental books. **25. The Rakes of Kildare: Second Warm-Up**

©2020 C. Harvey Publications All Rights Reserved.

92

The Blackberry Blossom Fiddle Book Score and Piano Accompaniment

26. The Rakes of Kildare

Page 36 in instrumental books.

Trad., arr. M. Harvey

©2020 C. Harvey Publications   All Rights Reserved.

The Blackberry Blossom Fiddle Book Score and Piano Accompaniment

©2020 C. Harvey Publications All Rights Reserved.

94 The Blackberry Blossom Fiddle Book Score and Piano Accompaniment

©2020 C. Harvey Publications All Rights Reserved.

The Blackberry Blossom Fiddle Book Score and Piano Accompaniment

©2020 C. Harvey Publications   All Rights Reserved.

Page 38 in instrumental books.

27. Big John McNeil: First Warm-Up

©2020 C. Harvey Publications   All Rights Reserved.

The Blackberry Blossom Fiddle Book Score and Piano Accompaniment

Page 39 in instrumental books. **28. Big John McNeil: Second Warm-Up**

©2020 C. Harvey Publications All Rights Reserved.

The Blackberry Blossom Fiddle Book Score and Piano Accompaniment

©2020 C. Harvey Publications All Rights Reserved.

100 The Blackberry Blossom Fiddle Book Score and Piano Accompaniment

©2020 C. Harvey Publications   All Rights Reserved.

The Blackberry Blossom Fiddle Book Score and Piano Accompaniment

©2020 C. Harvey Publications   All Rights Reserved.

102 — The Blackberry Blossom Fiddle Book Score and Piano Accompaniment

Page 42 in instrumental books.

30. Red-Haired Boy: First Warm-Up

©2020 C. Harvey Publications All Rights Reserved.

The Blackberry Blossom Fiddle Book Score and Piano Accompaniment

Page 43 in instrumental books.

31. Red-Haired Boy: Second Warm-Up

©2020 C. Harvey Publications All Rights Reserved.

32. Red-Haired Boy

Page 44 in instrumental books.

Trad., arr. M. Harvey

©2020 C. Harvey Publications   All Rights Reserved.

The Blackberry Blossom Fiddle Book Score and Piano Accompaniment 105

©2020 C. Harvey Publications   All Rights Reserved.

The Blackberry Blossom Fiddle Book Score and Piano Accompaniment

www.ingramcontent.com/pod-product-compliance
Lightning Source LLC
Chambersburg PA
CBHW081120080526
44587CB00021B/3675